BASHABI FRASER is a transna⸻   in
Edinburgh. She is a poet, edit⸻   ic.
Her awards include the IAS P⸻   in
2009. She has been widely publi⸻   ns
are *Scots Beneath the Banyan* ⸻ *⸻ ⸻⸻⸻ from Bengal* (2011); *From
the Ganga to the Tay* (an epic poem, 2009); *Bengal Partition Stories: An
Unclosed Chapter* (2006; 2008), *A Meeting of Two Minds: the Geddes
Tagore Letters* (2005) and *Tartan & Turban* (poetry collection, 2004).
Her research and writing traverse continents and cross borders and
boundaries. Bashabi is a Lecturer in English and Creative Writing at
Edinburgh Napier University. She is also a Royal Literary Fellow
based at the University of Dundee.

HERMANN RODRIGUES is an Edinburgh-based businessman and docu-
mentary photographer. He is planning to produce a book on Indians
living abroad globally. Right from his arrival in Edinburgh from
Jaipur, India, in the early Nineties he has been fascinated by the Asian
community settled in Scotland. He has been taking photographs and
collecting stories about Asians all over Scotland from Stornoway to
Dumfries. His work has been exhibited at the National Museums of
Scotland, St James Palace, Commonwealth Institute, National Library of
Scotland and has toured many cities of India as part of a British
Council Project. He lives in Edinburgh with his wife Abha and his son
Ashwin.

Ragas and Reels

Visual and Poetic Stories
of Migration and Diaspora

poems by *Bashabi Fraser*
with photographs by
Hermann Rodrigues

Luath Press Limited
EDINBURGH
www.luath.co.uk

First published 2012

ISBN: 978-1-908373-34-2

The paper used in this book is recyclable. It is made
from low-chlorine pulps produced in a low-energy, low-emissions
manner from renewable forests.

Printed and bound by
CPI Group (UK) Ltd, Croydon, CR0 4YY

Typeset in 10.5 point Sabon by
3btype.com

Bashabi: For Baba Neil and Rupsha
Hermann: For Abha and Ashwin

Foreword

BASHABI FRASER AND I are New Scots ourselves and are both interested in what being a 'New Scot' means – the life stories of other 'New Scots', of different generations, with issues of identity, conflict, displacement, relocation, acceptance (or otherwise), career etc. We both think of the subject historically – of Empire, of Scots returning from Empire, as well as the new diaspora from South Asia.

I have attended Bashabi's book launches and poetry readings and read her work over many years and appreciated the power of the poetry and its clarity of thought. These factors led naturally to this collaboration.

In her poems for this volume she has played with form with great dexterity. She has composed haiku, sonnets, tanka, the concrete poem, villanelle free verse, and uses couplets, tercets, quatrains and experiments with stanzaic variations which are effective in bringing each poem and its story alive.

This selection spans a long shared history between Scotland and South Asia – including how Scots brought India back with them. We chose a cross-section of 'New Scots' – from town and country, from different professions e.g., medicine, education, business, of different generations – to present a whole social fabric that is both representative and illuminating, illustrating their contribution to Scotland.

Hermann Rodrigues

The Fyrish Monument

A startled sun once saw its famous Gate
Of Negapatam become a victory arch
For General Hector Munro's
Regimen's historic march

The bemused sun watched
The General transform his countrymen
Into the progeny of Atlas
Carrying earth's burden

To the top of a hill at Fyrish
Recalling eastern grandeur
In a Monument whose empty cave
Archways gazed across a stranger

Landscape than they had witnessed –
Emptied of villages, their songs
And reels, replaced with the new music
Of winds echoing a bleating throng.

Legend has it that the stones
Were rolled down again
To be rebuilt by the General's men
To earn them a double bonus.

The arms hold up three massive
Doorways, with sentry stones on either side;
A witness is frozen at the centre
Who hails the sun that tips the tide.

Madras College, St Andrews

Oceans beckoned
The intrepid traveller
Across the Atlantic
And when the breakaway
Bugle broke the band –
There was another
Ocean waving
The man from St Andrews
To another shore
Where his countrymen
Had docked
And set anchor
For centuries more
To come.
The clergyman followed
The East India Company
Soldiers as the man
Of peace, ensuring
The future of their bairns
In an education regimen.
It was a baton
He passed on,
His class monitors

As tutors, to finish
A mammoth task
Against the tide
Of time, in a
Constant flame
Of undying light.

A name that has
Seen mutation
In its very
First tallow
Is the name
Dr Bell
Carried like a
Talisman
From his inspired
Days of improvisation
And commemorated
In his home town –
His Alma Mater
Where it remains
As a reminder
Of the possible –
Not a dream
But an institution
That ties the skeins

Of history's ironic themes
Of naming and claiming
When Tamil Nadu
And Chennai
Can claim kinship
With what was
Once a name
They donned
With fortitude.

Patna in the West

Nalanda, Pataliputra, Patna –
History shifts through earth's layers
As processions of voyagers course through
River ports and a hoary hinterland,
Till the entrance of the East India
Company entrepreneurs allows a love affair to grow
With the golden crop nurtured by the Ganga
Flowing through impatient plains.

The pearls were packed
In sacks and stamped
To roam across the world
As Patna Rice; the ancient
Continuity of India entering the
Scottish village arena, where
The cash crop embraced
The village in East Ayrshire,
Christening the primary school
With a name plucked from the
Gangetic Plains, now engraved
In every fold of life and carried
With pride in the crest
Of blazers by children
Who hold the legacy
Of a brand name that they
Owe to a nabob's wealth.

SIR COWASJI JEHANGIR, K.C.S.I.
THE PEABODY OF THE EAST
BY
THOMAS WOOLNER, Sculptor, Painter & Poet,
PRESENTED BY
SIR GEORGE BIRDWOOD, M.D.(Edin.)
K.C.I.E., C.S.I., LL.D.(Cantob & Edin.)

Sir Cowasji Jehangir Readymoney

The Peabody of the East
Gazes with quiet dignity
At any visitor pausing
To ponder on his serenity

Wondering how the integrity
Of marble captured the flowing
Folds and quiet dignity
Of this man whose overflowing

Wealth was channelled into sowing
Seeds in mental institutions,
Colleges and refuges for a growing
Population seeking restitution

Through work, when destitution
Threatened to crush their overflowing
Spirit, and Readymoney's institutions
And hospitals enfolded this growing

Populace in India's island city –
A Justice of the Peace
Whose grace and dignity
Woolner sculpted with artistic ease.

Sindbad at Stornoway

Sindbad, the itinerant merchant
Was renewed through time
In the hawker who
Began his journeys
In the land of the Indus
And pushed his boat
Across the kalapaani[1]
To the scattered Highland homes
And the island crofters
Till the voyage ended
At the edge of the Atlantic
In the Gaelic capital
Where the Celtic tongue now
Sits comfortably with Urdu
And women's hats
Are an easy transition
From head scarves in hues
As bright as tropical
Canaries, lining
Shelves and walls –
A multitude of magnum
Butterflies, to be lifted
For the holy day
When business is closed
And the world waits
As boats and planes
Sleep through the Sabbath,
Unwilling to disturb
The harbour and the airport
For it is here that
Sindbad the sailor
Has set down his anchor
At his journey's end
Blending in with the islanders
At Stornoway.

A Weekend Wedding in Stornoway

This is no politician's election campaign
On the sub-continent's rolling plains
This is a migrant flock flown in
To the Western Isles on a warm morning.

The father holds summer in his hand
The men wear Nehru's red rosebud
They came before Jinnah claimed their land
Which saw the exodus and the flood.

Here in the land of the wee free
They dominate the economy
The groom, a doctor trained on the mainland
Walks garlanded to his wedding band.

The bridal pair will move with grace
From school to school as the town feasts
Gathered to bless and celebrate
With this Gaelic speaking conglomerate.

Young Prithviraj[2]

Young Prithviraj came out from the east
He rode across continents and stopped in the west
He had crossed five rivers
That watered his land
He had witnessed lands severed
When the midnight clock turned –
The fate of millions, who then had to flee
To claim new homelands beyond the wide sea.

Prithviraj came riding through several decades
Three generations of chivalry, leading wedding parades
Today Prithviraj the third, trots into Leith
His white steed is gilded, crowned king and wreathed

The prince lifts a salute to his golden turban
Before lifting his bride to a bagpipe band
The saffron of India brightens turbans of men
In dark suits, who wait for the ceremony to begin.

Two boys

Silken turbans, flaming golden
Achkans[3] buttoned, bow-ties stiffened
Ushers steady, poised and ready
East and West are at their best
Side by side with charm and pride.

Breakfast – Scottish style

Crowned with gold
And turbaned pride
We're three wise kings
From the groom's side
While everyone is busy elsewhere
We sit down to our Scottish fare
The roti, chicken and *chana*[4] can wait
The wedding guests can arrive late
We are relaxed as we wash our hands
Like Maharajas in a splendid land
Where bacon, eggs, fries and toast
Are served to three kings as a feast.

The Golfers' Meet

The turf appears gilded in the soft twilight hour
The sky holds its breath as clouds wait to swirl.
The quartet of Singhs claims the last holes
At ease, yet deliberate in each swing of power.

The men followed the tide of colonial retreat
When nations fragmented, and millions were mourned
After one generation was buried or burnt and
Populations dispersed in victory and defeat.

Today they know the trees that grow roots
In this nation where peace has allowed enterprise
So each has found his own device
Floating his ship, and picking his fruit

Living in isolated distant turrets
Till one afternoon, by common consent
The four cornered brotherhood converges to vent
Its strength at the golf course as the horizon melts.

A Mirror Image Through Time

One still moment of calm commitment
The wedding garland promising plenty
The bridal crown and jewellery
Befitting youthful beauty, two slender youths
Poised for a future on another shore
Now caught in a studio before
Crowds of family and friends rush in again
To surround, applaud and restore
The social celebration of two lives
Conjoined and ready for the unknown.

Decades intervene. The contours alter.
Colour pervades a private hedgerow
Replacing a private studio wall
A patio paved with proportionate precision
Provides a solid resting ground
From the carpet of uncertain dreams.
Western masculinity still prevails,
Only more pronounced now in the tartan shirt
And the tweed cap, while the woman
Retains the pride of tradition, as the bride of yesterday
Stands in relaxed composure, her intricate
Embroidery draping her eastern confidence –
At home, as one page of her life has turned
To another in a continuity that only history
Will understand in its persistent repetition.

Eastern Grace

He followed the footprints of the 'Guinea Lady' –
His Great Aunt, who expended gold coins
On the porters at Victoria Quay.

He was mistaken as the Grecian owner
Of his Greek restaurant and in his crafts
Shop, as an East European entrepreneur.

She could never be mistaken for what she was
The elegant lady from the sub-continent –
Always in her sari, exuding eastern grace.

While the Royal Mile moved through light and dark
Moments with business spaces changing hands,
Their Eastern Crafts remained a constant landmark

Where artistically crafted woodwork and china,
Magic spun fabrics and burnished brass
Flaunted the exotic to the spellbound foreigner

Combing the High Street on bright summer days
To enter the portals of this recess to beauty
And marvel with Scotsmen at eastern grace.

The Bangladeshi Gentleman

The day looks promising
The sun is out in full glory
Spilling over the back garden
With reckless plenitude.
It stirs memories of frolic
On the foothills where teagardens
Caress the Sylhet landscape.
Today, dressed to match
The regal sun, it is time
To hold court against
The circle of sun-showered bushes
Enthroned in a colonial
Basket chair lifted from the tropics –
It is the right moment
To re-enact a still from
Another world, seconds before
The sun, like an eccentric
Monarch, retreats from public
View in a country where it
Holds only rare audiences.

The Professor in his Garden

Last September, the bulbs were dipped
Into the loosened soil and not forgotten
But watched and watered with protective
Earnestness, and with the loyalty of tended love
They have sprouted in the mild surprise of spring warmth
Into a multitude of butterfly colours.
One tree needs doctoring, its eager shade
Providing a cloistered arbour for the battling blossoms,
While underneath, the grass grows with passionate abandon
Encouraged by repeated April showers. It is time
To cut back the branching canopy,
Mow down the invading grass and
Dig up the soil for fresh beds for a new display
Of summer visitors. On a sunny Sunday
Afternoon, the spade is all abuzz
With officious business – under the
Expert guidance of its focussed handler
As the Professor takes a break in his garden.

The Doctor at Home

The Bengal lawyer
Saw former colonies
Find prosperity

In a brave free world
Through delegations he led
For his new nation.

His daughter followed
A tradition of Indian
Doctors in Scotland

Taking another
Route that others had taken
From her father's land.

Here in her garden
She has seen her life blossom
Just as she has coaxed

Health to bloom in those
She helps when she is not sun
Kissed and relaxing.

The Laird of Lesmahagow

There is something about Scotland –
Its rugged hills and islands
That seem to touch the soul
Which follows a deep call
Magnetic in its pull,
Hypnotic beyond rules.

So the Londoner of real estate
Cruising in his Rolls Royce
Finds that he is bound by fate
To listen to this beckoning voice
And leave all one day with his Swiss lass
To adopt Scotland's sea-sprayed grass.

And is this nationalistic mood
The migrant buys one island
Which he names after the bard
And himself becomes a Scottish laird
Where he sees his garden grow
In the bonnie toon of Lesmahagow.

And once when floods came without warning,
Invading Paisley's surprised homes
The laird opened the castle's rooms
To families one memorable morning
Guests who stayed to taste the vitality
Of spontaneous Punjabi hospitality.

The laird lives and walks today
With his dog along the bay
A turbaned Sikh with his scabbard
A warrior and a Scottish laird
His clan tartan in green and blue
Reflects a shared history now renewed.

The Perfect Smile

He says I'm restless
Like a cloud
He says I'll get lost
In this crowd.

I think he has
A sense of guilt
For not wearing
A tartan kilt.

But I'm ready
If your hand's steady
And before he whisks me from this spot
You must take the perfect shot

It's he who is restless
And he blames *me*!
I think he's jealous
Because *you* like me.

Can I ask you to dance with me –
He cannot hold me eternally
I'll join you soon on the floor
Whirling round in Strip the Willow.

I'll take your hand and be your gallant
Dancing the Dashing White Sergeant.

Ashwin and his Scottish Granny

It is story time today,
And we are sitting comfortably
On Granny's spacious knee
And what is it to be?
Bob the Builder's story
Of constructing a home
For a family
That has come
From the pink city
Of palaces to this one
Of brown stone?

Or will it be
Of the whistling dapper
Thomas the Tank Engine
Wearing his cheeky grin
Who has passengers
With messages
That they will take today
To Inverkeithing, Kilmarnock,
Perth or Abertay?

But will Gran have time enough
To have both stories read
Before mums and dads return
To say it's time for bed?

Black and White

I am a panther on the prowl
From a jungle now set free
I haunt the Scottish landscape
From Dundee to Portree
Do you see how black and white
Blend in so well on me?
Do I scare you with my fierce glance
Are you ready to flee?

Graduation

The solid circularity of McEwan Hall
Affirms the stolid reality of history
Repeating itself, a cliché that never seems
To surprise each new family that appears
Like jubilant actors after a feisty show,
Standing proud and sunshine-filled
To an ecstatic applause that only they hear
Amidst the competing pride of achievement –
Posing on that stage before they are replaced
By other trios of flanking proud parents
Propping the red cylinder-holding graduate,
The rainbow hue of nationalities
Confirming the tribes that will always come in new waves
With ambitions to replace old generations
In a circle of avowed determination to
Renew a search for a foothold to fame.

Literature that travelled East

Macaulay's Minute in 1835
Brought English as an imposition
On the history of a proud nation
With its 3,000 year old literary life.

And with it came the gift of words
That would open riveted doors
To philosophers and bards
Speaking from another shore.

Writers like Orwell and Forster
Travelled to the East and served,
Challenging imperial constructs
Questioning the given facts.

And this fresh light of vision ignited
A reappraisal on all sides.
Wars intervened, the glamour subsided
And a new perspective weighed the tide.

And with this tide the east now turned
In a counter journey to the west
And at the end of this sojourn
It found the chalice of its quest.

The portals of Old College
With its ancient solid embrace
Now accepts the sincere homage
Born of an eastern scholar's grace

Her inner resilience hidden by an outer fragility
Which has bonded with Orwell's cry for liberty
As she now stands with a scholar's easy dignity
Defying the old shackles of her nation's history.

From Salisbury Crags

Here the sky is the limit
That the Salisbury crags
Can contemplate

Against the verge of Arthur's seat
Where the corbies rest, rage
Or meditate

Upon the cityscape unfolded
With castle, spires, domes and towers
That gravitate

Towards the sea and stop in time
To gaze where once the Thane of Fife ruled
His hilly state

That witnesses the Forth's embrace
Which laps the poet's present muse
And chosen fate.

Against MacDiarmid's Plaque

The rain has left a moist kiss
Reviving the terraced grass.
The hill bends down as if to slide
The houses perched on its side
A field has slipped down the slope
And reflecting its tropical sheen
An old dance form in golden hope
Unfolds against replenished green.

The dancer's rhythmic feet freeze into pose –
In time with the tilting earth
The armadillo's spikes rise
Behind the stones' circled girth.
His shadow hovers over words
That welcome his passing gift
Of homage paid to the bard,
Healing past time-blurred rifts.

The Dancer

The sitar's[5] strings tingle the audience to attention
Like rain water embracing a willing stream
The tablas'[6] tehai[7] is the cue for the vision
In turquoise and blue
To spin onto stage –
A glorious globe
Rotating with freedom,
Pulsating with life.
Slender arms reach out
In graceful abandon –
So swift, you nearly miss
Each magic sleight.
The ghungrus[8] pick up
The reverberation
Of creative variations
In a tarana's[9] refrain,
Eternalised now
In a hypnotic moment
The movement held still –
One peacock hand raised
Another beckoning
The lips appealing –
Has she seen a vision
That radiates her expression?

The Singer on a Scottish Slope

The hills have come alive
With the sound of music
Rippled from the veena[10]
And rolled in sonorous folds
Across the grassy slope
Where the heather holds
The sky with its mesmeric
Purple charm. Here the singer
Finds a place under the sun
To send her echoing ragas[11]
Across the crest, over the loch –
Her sari fluttering with amorous
Abandon to the wind that
Waits as a messenger, willing to
Lift up her notes and scatter
Them across Arthur's Seat
Over the Firth to Fife
In notes that will soothe the soul
Of the Thane's slaughtered wife
Letting old ghosts rest at last
With a joy instilling breath.

Ragas and Reels

The rollicking rhythm from Highland Springs
Matched with classical ankle bells,
Lifts the mists from burn and brae
Disperses monsoon clouds away
The quick step tunes, with urgency
Spur the dancers to a frenzy
Of hypnotic movement, with precision and verve
Compelling eyes, sharp turns and curves
Mudras[12] like magic, swift wave of hand
Feet beat the tala[13], challenging the band
The floodlights shower beams, the footlights applaud
This vision of fusion from home and abroad.

At a Fashion Show

This is no temple with goddesses
In every alcove draped
In rainbow silks
Waiting for our homage.

They have not stepped
On to earth to stroll
At ease, beneath
Sunbeams on glittering sand.

They are the vibrant
Moving images of time
They glisten in the spotlight
They are glamour's queens

They have brought their
Spices with them
In their swinging walk
Their delectable glance.

They can swirl past –
A whiff of hypnotic
Ardour breezing from
Their anchal[14] wings.

They can turn away
Daring eyes to linger
Or stand, holding
The moment in tranquil splendour.

They have inherited
The silken thread
The dusky romance
In their sunrise song

They beckon their mothers
To join their victory march
They wear beauty as a badge
In the land where they belong.

From Lahore to West Lothian

She comes from the intimate streets of Lahore
Which was Kipling's playground as a boy,
The same city where Kim sat astride a cannon,
Conscious of his position of authority
As an orphan of parents of colonial lineage.

She stands at ease before Hopetoun House
The seat of Lord Linlithgow, the Viceroy
Of India when Lahore was the home for
Many who were forced to leave the city
And find new roots in a post-border age.

But she is a post-midnight child, who left
As education became a beckoning flame
That drew her from Lahore's historic
Walls to encounter another history
That is intricately woven in a fabric

Of overlapping identity. She brings
With her a confidence that has become
Her hallmark, the psychiatric consultant
Who wears designs with elegance, her mastery
Complete, as her children fit into this new rubric.

Caledonia, Persia, India and Rio

They met in the corridors of learning
He had seen the noon sun empty
The echoing spaces of the Red Fort yearning
To retrieve the imperial days of plenty

He stood now on the banks of a river
That had sent ambitious sons to battle
On rolling plains where a sun they had never
Experienced, shone with luminous ardour, testing their mettle.

She stood face to face in the metropole
That had dominated a network of humanity
They met in a free world, their global role
United to claim through names, regions and cities

Caledonia, Persia, India and Rio
Have seen the old world merge with the new.

The Restauranteur

Corus is the steel bridge
That has spanned across
Continents to bring together
Two nations in a world of
Free enterprise, as Tata
Steps in to keep the furnace aglow.
Metaphors mix, with the red heat
Of metal becoming the slogan
Of curries cooked for the host
Nation to its expectation,
Sold with aplomb by a Bollywood
Star. His name is Khan
And he is no terrorist, but
A Bangladeshi entrepreneur
Whose millions in taxes keep
Scotland's finance alight
With the promise that satisfies
Palates with attractive returns.

A Garden of Flavours

This is where the curry leaves grow
Lined by coriander in neat rows
Bay leaves, cinnamon, chillies sprout
While turmeric waits to be dug out
There are cumin seeds for jeera[15] rice
And saffron that comes at its own price
Fenugreek's aroma fills the sense
The gourds' plump fervour spills over the fence
Potatoes wait to be discovered in nooks
Like uncharted lands, by a Captain Cook
Tomatoes blush from their glass abode
As the eastern chef notes their mood
Nurtured in his tropical Eden
Creating flavours to capture a nation.

Suruchi for Guid Taste

– *A menu ye cannae beat* –

Suruchi means guid taste
Where yo'll find the brawest o' the East
In a by-ordiner feast.
For a guid taste o' Scotland wi' Indian sterter
There's vegetarian haggis in gram flooer batter,
Salmon tikka grillit wi spice tae flavour
An skewert kebab, in a braw feast tae savour.
For the heatsome and hailsom o a' that is Indian
There's licht stappit samosas an' cheese stappit nan
Sonsie dauds o' jalfrezie chicken
Dentie herbs on sappie on praans.
But the ultimate o' curries ye cannae forgit
Is Sooth Indian chicken wi' coconut –
That Nirvana that has a root
In wha's authentic an knackie
In a menu that stan's oot
For being cannie and quirkie.

Building the Bodyline

The scaffolding is the backdrop
To the story of conservation,
Renovation and construction
As the city shapes and reshapes
Its skyline and façade
Facilitated by the muscle
Of dedicated energy
That toughens the sinews
And one labour leads to another
Fruit, building the perfect body
That prompts the applause
Of an approving population.

Football in the Meadows

The grass is disturbed in its depths
Responding with gratitude to the shower
That throws up the mud from its green carpet sheen
Kicked with ardour in the ball which encompasses
The rivalry of east and west coast
As Edinburgh and Glasgow confront
One another in diverse strips
In Bangladeshi teams
Loyal to the castle city
Or the city of engineers
Divided with energetic vigour
– Just for today.

Eid[16] Outdoors

This amazing stretch of green
Is like the tropical maidan
They call the Meadows
Breathing free in a spacious city.
And while the Mosque takes shape
Brick by brick, beyond the trees –
This is the prime place
For Mecca to be evoked
On a day when Allah is merciful
And a congregation gathers
To turn east in unison
And pray to celebrate Eid.

The Candidate

Mo Rizvi, Mo Rizvi
The election poster reaches out
Mo Rizvi, Mo Rizvi
A moment held in multiple shots.

One brown petal on a cold white bough
One sharp image in a wide white space
One lone voice whispering from the margins
One man's ballot speaking for his race.

In this game of numbers
His was not to win
But the subaltern had spoken
For an era to begin.

Friday Prayers at Glasgow's Central Mosque

The
Muezzin's
Call has been a bugle
Alert for the two thousand
Who now gather on the south bank
Of the Clyde and bend in disciplined unison
For the Zuhr Salah[17], facing the magnetic power of
Mecca, confident of the sun's certainty while
The interior lights shine, the fans frozen
For now, ready to whir into action
As the congregation prays, led by
The Imam in devout solidarity.

Student Monk

The forgotten land of the planet's plateau
Is where great rivers are conceived
The snow table is their alpha
In a land of the bereaved.

From this pristine point of inception
Springs a dignity and grace
From abstinence and contemplation
Flows a life stream through harsh days

The saffron robes are threads that tied
The plateau to a sub-continent
As Buddha's followers sought to hide
Far from the storms of discontent.

The lotus petals enfold the truth of knowledge
In their ample arms
Which monks seek as a privilege
Replacing their bowl of alms.

The curtain can now descend
Between them and their landlocked world
The table lamp can glow on books
With Buddhist serenity unfurled.

Inside Samye ling

Deep inside the burnished hall
Amidst the ornate wooden honeycomb
Of quiet treasures, sits the Compassionate One
Contemplating in the silence as the gongs
Wait like watchful sentinels, walling in
The monks at prayer, their scriptures
Idle, letting the muted meditating air
Stand still in this sanctuary that rests
Comfortably on the undulations of the Borders
Having arrived without flourish
On an invisible magic carpet
Straight from the land of Zhongs
In the eastern Himalayas, to its
Chosen place of tranquil refuge.

The Hindu Temple in Leith

They each had their own special shrine
In a temple dedicated to a single deity,
Unless they were inseparable consorts
Like Radha and Krishna or Shiva and Parvati.
But that was in a vast land with ample space and time
For 330 million gods and goddesses
To have their place and shrine.

But here they have graciously entered
In a group to stand in a motley crowd
For new arrivals to worship
In this unifying church which devotees have transformed
With gifts of saris draped around in a canopy
That protects the heavenly host
Who in turn look upon with benevolent tolerance
At men and women entering through separate
Doors and congregating to celebrate every Jayanti[18]
And Puja[19], not as they did, ringing one bell
At a single open doorway, in the land
Where it all began, but recreated in new finery
With Bramha's blessings and Vishnu's protection,
While Shiva meditates in a dreaming trance –
For this is a world he wills and lets flow
Like a new river from his knotted hair
Accompanying a migrant stream
To pray, preserve and persevere
And perchance to dream …

Durga Puja in Glasgow

Goddess – how long will stay?
Goddess – you will have to go away!
Goddess – how long can you rest?
Goddess – you will have to be immersed!

At first Durga came,
As a borrowed deity
From Belsize Park's
Bengali Community.

As a work of beauty
She graced the Art Centre
At Kingston Bridge
In Glasgow

And moved like a
Visiting artist,
Her gracious presence
Endowed

As a blessing to
Adelphi High School,
Then at the Palace of Art
At Belahouston Park

Till she felt she could
Linger longer
At Namdev Centre,
Continuing her work

Of healing and solace
For the hundreds
Who thronged for
Five festive days

To her resplendent
Presence, a single mother
For now, an intrepid
Traveller from the haze

Of Kailash[20], having
Embarked on a
Hazardous journey
Along the mighty Ganga[21]

With her four children.
She is our Victoria
The lion rider
From heaven

Flanked by the second generation
In Saraswati providing knowledge, and
Kartik the warrior
God of love and courage

Lakshmi, the gracious guardian
Of our homes' comfort zone
And Ganesh, the fine diner –
The friend of businessmen.

From Namdev Centre
Durga then moved
To Cooper Institute
A venue she has approved

With adapting alacrity.
She has taken to flights,
Covering sky miles
On a cargo plane.

She has allowed
A make-up artist
To touch up her radiant smile
That lights this cold terrain

She symbolizes Victory
Knowledge, Nurture, Grace
She brings together a community
In homage and in praise.

From 1981 she
Has faithfully arrived
Every year to Glasgow
In splendour and in pride

Of having conquered
Evil to save
A suffering world
Where she can set the
Cymbals clanging
And see the incense burned
Where anjali[22] will bring
Flowers at her feet
And arati[23] will
Light a flame
To circle to the beat
Of a distant drum
On another shore
To which her devotees
Will turn
When autumn leaves
Their door.

The Gurdwara in Leith

Where the city stops at an ocean's brink
Once ships set sail or docked to rest
They paused to ponder on the kingdom
Looming through the morning mists.

Bhai, Landa, Kasbia, Potwal
Ronde, Rathour, Sheber, Digpal
Names repeated like a mantra
From the cradle of their yatra[24]

Unified in prayer, they had sought
Tenement flats to pray and meet
Till St Thomas opened doors to greet
A community from a divided state.

The khalsa symbol of balance, power and continuity
Now meditates on the pinnacle of a dockside city.

It's time to Bhangra!

Plentiful harvests release the tension
Of labouring months under an unforgiving sun
Then the land yields to its proverbial fame
As the supplier of milk and honey
In golden wheat sheaves that are turned over
For a population now jubilant with success.
It's time to bhangra – that masculine vigour
That sets shoulders pulsating to the heady beat
Of the dholki[25], the arms raised with sheer abandon
The feet kicking the dust, tracing freedom's steps
Challenging the very air with lusty leaps
Fingers clicking, hands clapping, heads flicking –

The bhangra has now seeped into the imagination
Of a sub-continent, the expression of jubilation
The rhythms rocking across a vast land,
Rolling over the seas with a fresh harvest
So the wave that once brought the Punjab to Scottish shores.
As itinerant merchants, are replaced by a new generation
Of the roving technology savvy globe trotters
At home with a jetsetting wanderlust to work
With contracts, to meet and dance the bhangra
With gusto on Diwali night in a closed room
And then pick up their bags to shoot across the sky
Where their next contract lies, carrying the celebratory
Rhythm in their very pulsebeat as they embrace
A multinational world of interwoven interests.

Of Dreamboats and Surfers

Miralles'[26] dreamboat floats
Like a surprised vision,
Upturned on the edge
Of the city, greeted by hill slopes
And saluted by stiff crags –
Its postmodern glass
And tropical bamboo
Mirroring and tethering
Time's flow in its renewing
Capability, its flanking
Design matched by the web
The spreads out and captures
Net surfers who drift in
To navigate this new age
Political ship for the world
To come on board and view,
And once their charted seas
Are navigated with ease
The surfers will weave their way
To flag off other boats
Along fresh cyber routes.

Wee Cumbrae

Sea birds have nested here
Lapped by the tide of the Clyde
The memory of Cromwell's army
Dimmed for generations, as Robert II's
Castle stands in ruins and the lighthouse
Is the last beacon that signals
Its presence and whispers to green Great
Cumbrae. The Wee one's rocky reality
Is echoed in its far flung Hebridean cousins.

One cloudless day, the birds
Were disturbed by ripples of bagpipes
Piercing the layers of silence
As a procession ribboned across
The isle. The sheep stood amazed as a saffron-clad
Yogi saluted the island's hard vigour
In a startling sky-reaching handstand
Symbolising the ambitious feat
That aimed at the zenith
And promised to bring many marching feet
From across the world to a corner
Of meditative restoration, now renamed
And reclaimed as Peace Island
By new migrants determined
To build new nests, transforming
The territory of the wind and the tide
To a centripetal force forging new encounters.

Vellore in Scotland

The city that has seen dynasties rise and fall
And was Vijayanagar Kingdom's crown jewel
With its fort as a symbol of a captor's power
Has transferred its name to Falkirk's fields
In a road that roams with quiet ease through
A village that has not dreamt of its heritage
As a hairdresser proudly scans the horizon
For the customer drawn by the sign to her trade.
The bustling city near old Madras, baptises
A mansion, a cottage and a road in a nation
Where it can slumber and dream of its many
Splendoured bygone days.

Jura Whisky

An Acrostic –

Just where the tides of life ebb and flow
Under the mercy of a cavalier wind
Roving with the whiplash of horsepower rain,
Anchors the island where Orwell dwelt.

Willing the world to wish him well as Jura
Harboured his loves and bones in post-eastern days.
In time the east has braced this western isle
Signalling a reversed trade route which now
Kindles blended brands to leave a glass
Yurt, as Whyte & Mackay and Jura roam air miles.

The Malankara Church

St Thomas the Syrian has been claimed
As the disciple who in the first century came
To lead the Malabar Nasrani in Jesu's name

Till the Portuguese arrived at the southern coast
Bringing with them the Catholic host
In a tug-of-faiths which was settled at a cost.

Today the Syrian Orthodox choose to congregate
With the Catholics from their native state
As Malayalam is the bonding thread that unites

A group gathered to sing, pray and feast
On the last Sunday every month, with their priest
From London, offering the Eucharist.

The seventeenth century tensions have long been dissolved
And the Pope's new dispensation has resolved
All tensions in this resplendent deputy of God.

Index

The Fyrish Monument was erected in 1782 at Easter Ross on Fyrish Hill under the direction of the General, Sir Hector Munro to resemble the Gate of Negapatam, near Madras (now Chennai), where the General won a significant battle in 1781 as a General in the British Army.

The Madras College at St Andrews uses the system of education invented by Revd. Dr Andrew Bell (1753–1832). Dr Bell was a Scottish clergyman, whose task was to educate the children of soldiers in the East India Company at Madras. The method he invented consisted of trained older students, called 'monitors', teaching younger learners, which became known as the 'Madras method'.

Patna in the West: Patna is a village in East Ayrshire, built in 1802 by William Fullarton for his coal mining workers. Fullarton's father had served in Patna for the East India Company. The name became the brand name of rice that the Scottish nabob bought from the plains in the hinterland of Patna on the Ganges, and packaged and sold globally. Patna Primary School commemorates a link provided by a name and a shared history, and the school crest still bears the name.

Sir Cowasji Jehangir Readymoney, CSI (1812–1878), also known as The Peabody of the East, was a Parsi philanthropist from Bombay (now Mumbai). He made his fortune as a broker to two prominent European firms, became a commissioner of income tax and set up and helped many charitable institutions in Bombay, including hospitals, colleges and provided support for the destitute. His statue by Thomas Woolner stands near the bottom of a great staircase at Old College of the University of Edinburgh.

Sindbad at Stornoway is a tribute to the descendents of Buta Ahmed. Ahmed made his way to Stornoway as a door-to-door salesman in the 1930s. In time, the family set down roots in Stornoway and is one of the biggest employers in the Isle of Lewis capital. The Sardar and Sons Superstore is a landmark in the town. This poem shows a member of this community in his popular hat shop in the town.

A Weekend Wedding in Stornoway marks a wedding in the British Pakistani family when the school halls were kept open over the weekend so that the bridal pair could visit each community group at a South Asian style wedding feast to which the whole town was invited.

Young Prithviraj commemorates the wedding of a Leith Sikh. The Sikhs of Leith have lived there since the 1960s. See endote to the reference to Prithviraj for the story behind the historic figure.

Two boys captures two young Sikhs dressed up for a wedding celebration.

Breakfast – Scottish Style shows Sikh boys enjoying true Scottish fare on the morning of a Sikh wedding.

The Golfers' Meet shows four Sikhs who have all built their separate business empires and, at a rare moment, meet for a relaxed game of golf.

A Mirror Image through Time shows two photographs of a British Pakistani couple. The lady came as a bride to Britain in 1968 and later moved to Edinburgh with her husband. She set up the famous brand name of Mrs Unis's naan bread and is a respected entrepreneur in the hospitality trade, giving employment and dignity to women workers. The two photographs commemorate the dreams and hopes of a newly married couple and the easy grace of success in later years.

Eastern Grace: Their forebears had made the sea journey to Britain, so 'bilayet' (foreign land, signifying Britain) was not a strange land for them, where they brought the same goods the colonizers had once travelled to their lands for, bringing them to the doorstep of Scotland's population. Full of enterprise and business acumen, they floated many ventures, including a Greek restaurant that did brisk business. Their Eastern Crafts' shop is what remain indelible in the memory of their faithful customers for its reliable location where one could encounter beautiful objects and hospitality imbued with true eastern grace.

The Bangladeshi Gentleman is a man who has brought the flavours of the land watered by the river Padma to a Scottish clientele. The subject of the photograph has been the Honorary Bangladeshi Consul from Sylhet. Sylhet is a district in Bangladesh where many Scottish Bangladeshis originate. In this captured moment, he sits in his Scottish back garden, enjoying a rare sunny afternoon.

The Professor in his Garden shows the busy academic relaxing when he is not thinking of his many research projects as Professor of Public Health at the University of Edinburgh.

The Doctor at Home: begins with the journey a Bengali barrister and legal advisor, made to his Irish wife's city, Dublin, from where he represented Ireland at the Judiciary Committee of the EEC. His daughter, with the dual heritage of two colonial countries, is a GP in the National Health Service which has had many doctors from India serving the Scottish population. She has four sons who are proud Scots.

The Laird of Lesmahagow, Baron Singh, moved to Scotland in 1987 from London, accompanied by his Swiss wife. Originally from Lahore, he has embraced Scotland and holds the title of Laird of Lesmahagow, has his own Singh tartan and has bought an island. He has named it Burns Island, paying his own tribute to the Scottish bard. Baron Singh has translated Burns's Scots poems into Punjabi.

The Perfect Smile of the little boy in a kilt was taken many years ago, for the little Scotsman in the photograph now has a flourishing dentist's practice.

Ashwin and his Scottish Granny shows little Ashwin with his adopted Scottish granny and his little Scottish friend, spending one of many memorable storytelling evenings together when parents were away. Ashwin is now at university, a skilled guitarist and a vocalist who specialises in fusion music of east and west.

Black and White shows a little South Asian girl enjoying face painting. This photograph is part of Hermann's series with the same title.

Graduation: First generation parents who have both had successful careers, now take pride in their second generation offspring's achievement on graduation day at Edinburgh University.

Literature that Travelled East shows a PhD student at Old College, studying George Orwell's work for a doctoral thesis in English at Edinburgh University.

From Salisbury Crags: Here the poet can stand and have a bird's eye view of the city of Edinburgh, which is her current Muse.

Against McDairmid's Plaque shows a student from India, doing a Master's degree, but not in dance – though he is an accomplished Kathak exponent.

The Dancer shows a second generation British Indian, who is a scientist and, at the same time, an accomplished Kathak dancer.

A Singer on a Scottish Slope portrays the founder of Sangeet Mala, a South Asian Choir. The singer, who has a mellifluous voice, has worked to popularise South Asian songs across Scotland, singing with Scottish bands in fusion events.

Ragas and Reels captures a dance company called India Alba, founded in Edinburgh by a Bharatnatyam dancer, which has a multi-cultural troupe and performs all over Scotland. This particular photograph depicts a fusion piece with Indian classical dance being performed to a Scottish reel.

At a Fashion Show depicts a fundraising event for a charity which raises money for a girls' orphanage on the sub-continent. The models are second generation high school or university students, wearing their mothers' and aunties' saris with the confidence and pride of being British Asians.

From Lahore to West Lothian: shows a consultant psychiatrist at home in Scotland in her multiple roles as medical expert, wife of a Scot and mother of Scottish children, wearing a Karen Miller designer dress with the ease of an international citizen.

Caledonia, Persia, India and Rio are the names of four siblings, whose parents are from east and west, having met as students at University in Britain.

The Restauranteur: Around 95 per cent of the 'Indian' restaurants in Scotland are owned/manned by Bangladeshis. 'Curry' has become a national dish, cooked to suit the local taste. The Tata company of India has bought Corus, so British Steel under Indian ownership has revived a flagging company. The mixed metaphors become apparent as the 'strength' of Indian cuisine is shown to be made for the Scottish palate by a Bangladeshi who poses like a 'Bollywood' star in front of a billboard. The subject of the photograph also acts in 'Bollywood' films in swashbuckling roles when Mumbai film companies come to shoot films against the Scottish landscape.

A Garden of Flavours: The story of a man offering fine dining at his restaurants with herbs and spices from his own garden, echoes the story of many jute technologists who came to study in Dundee's College of Jute Technology from what was East Pakistan, and then found themselves stranded as political refugees during the Independence War which led to the formation of Bangladesh in 1971. These students from middle class, well educated families, had to abandon their studies as jute technology shut down, funds from 'home' dried up and the students had to look for new means of survival in a country where they had not arrived with any intentions of settling down. The Dundee Bangladeshis remain an enlightened group, having built educational links with Bangladesh as they have initiated a programme with Ninewells Hospital where visiting doctors receive training and contribute to reducing child mortality in Bangladesh.

Suruchi for Guid Taste: Suruchi is a restaurant which was originally set up by a Bangladeshi entrepreneur, and has seen transformation and transmutation under its current owner, who is the photographer in this book. It holds festivals of food, moving from state to state on the sub-continent, inviting its clientele to sample the 'real' India with its regional variety. Suruchi has expanded to open 'Suruchi Too' and has introduced fusion cooking in haggis pakoras and salmon tikka. It offers a Scots menu which reflects its fusion dishes of Scottish produce cooked with South Asian flavours. Suruchi has hosted the launch of a Scots dictionary.

Building the Bodyline is the story of a builder who contributes to the developers' business during the day and in his free time, doubles up as a body building champion, representing Scotland in international matches.

Football in the Meadows: Bangladeshi teams from Edinburgh and Glasgow confront each other in a game of football, echoing the old rivalries between the two cities in serious opposition.

Eid Outdoors: This photograph was taken when the mosque was in the process of being built, and Muslims celebrated Eid in the Meadows of Edinburgh.

The Candidate: Mo Rizvi stood in the local elections when there were no brown faces visible on the political scene. He lost, but he did make a point by his very candidature. His daughter became a Councillor later.

Friday Prayers at Glasgow's Central Mosque: The Central Mosque in Glasgow can allow 2,000 devotees to pray together and is also a thriving community centre.

Student Monk shows a visiting student from Tibet, who has seen his proud nation being absorbed by China as one of her states.

Inside Samye ling shows A Buddhist monastery in the Borders/ the Southern Uplands of Scotland. The monastery is a tranquil place, redolent of Zhongs in the Himalayas, whose architecture is reflected in this edifice.

The Hindu Temple in Leith: Housed in a Church, unlike the temples in India, which are dedicated to one deity (or to two if they are consorts), the Hindu temple in Leith in Edinburgh, like most British temples, welcomes multiple gods and goddesses, giving the migrant Hindu an opportunity to pray to the deity of her/his choice.

Durga Puja in Glasgow has the chequered history of most religious groups in Scotland, having small beginnings and moving from venue to venue as the congregation grown with time. Begun by the local Indian Bengali community, with the first images borrowed from England, Durga Puja attracts and welcomes South Asians and the mainstream community, offering a free delicious vegetarian meal over five days of Durga, the Mother Goddesses's ceremonial worship (puja) to all visitors, and accepting donations from visitors. Meals are prepared by the community members and even on evenings when the visitors number 500, no one is turned away. Now the images are transported by flights, straight from Kolkata's district of master craftsmen.

The Gurdwara in Leith: Leith has seen the settlement of Sikhs, who have lived there for four generations, as many of them found themselves without a country when Partition drove a decisive line that made them aliens in the land of their ancestors. The Sikh temple in Leith began in a small tenement flat and like the Hindu temple in the same area, is now housed in a former church.

It's Time to Bhangra shows a new group of itinerants – the IT personnel who come to Scotland as their firms work with Scottish companies with contracts. This is a new set from a new India, with the confidence of the educated and skilled worker, which has no intention of settling down, but will pick up its bags and move on to other countries as the globalised market demands. For now it meets and dances the Bhangra to celebrate Diwali in a hall in Scotland.

Of Dreamboats and Surfers portrays a group of IT personnel from the sub-continent which works on the Scottish Parliament's website and is housed in the avant garde Parliament building.

Wee Cumbrae has been bought by the powerful Poddar couple and renamed Peace Island, with the purpose of welcoming world pilgrims to join meditation retreats with the famous Indian Yogi, Swami Ramdev. The photograph commemorates the inauguration of the island as a meditation and Ayurvedic centre.

Vellore in Scotland: The photograph shows the sign to the village which bears a name taken from a historic city in India. Vellore House and Vellore Cottage (in Ballater) also signify the colonial link.

Jura Whisky: is produced by a company that is one of the largest in Scotland, has a huge market in India and is owned by an Indian businessman.

The Malankara Church takes its name after the Malankara Syrian Orthodox Church in Kerala, whose followers are known as St Thomas Christians or the Nasrani (reference to Nazareth) Christians.

It is popularly believed that their conversion dates back to 52AD. In India, many Syrian Orthodox Christians were forcibly converted to Catholicism under the Portuguese around 1540. Once Portuguese power waned in the colonial history of the sub-continent, some Catholics reverted to their old Syrian Orthodox faith. Today, however, the two groups not only live amicably together but also intermarry. The church on Ferry Road in Edinburgh, which both groups attend, reflects a historic common root and continuing association. The current Bishop has a special dispensation from the Pope to hold a joint mass for his Catholics and Syrian Orthodox congregation.

Afterword

I ENCOUNTERED Hermann Rodrigues' work 15 years ago and have since been fascinated by the human interest that has inspired his subject choice. As he himself has told me, when he first came to Scotland, he was moved by the beauty of the Scottish landscape and its historic urban complexes and castles. However, when it came to the point of recording Scotland as Hermann saw it through the small lens, it was not Scotland's lochs, hills and glens, her heritage buildings or proud city skylines that he wanted to capture. What inevitably drew his attention was a 'broon' face in this predominantly white society. Questions followed – why had this particular individual come here and when, how did this community grow and what are its achievements and contribution to Scottish society? And each portrait had a story to tell, intricate in its complexity, while encapsulating the history of whole communities.

I have seen Hermann Rodrigues' work in various exhibitions round the country and encountered an audience's appreciation of an unfolding peoples' story. It was this interest in personal life stories that brought us together to collaborate in a book that would tell of individual lives and community stories through visual images matched by words.

I have not used italics for Scots and Indian words in the poems, but have provided Endnotes with explanations for most of the words from the sub-continent.

Moments and memories held layers of history which have not been a one-way journey and do not form just a recent phenomenon. The colonial skein weaves these stories together as place names from the sub-continent find their way to villages, roads, houses, structures and even in an education system – that began in the east and was brought by the travelling Scot from India, to surprise the Scottish landscape with names that have their roots elsewhere. But here they have grown new roots and come to stay. While place names have travelled from east to west, a sense of belonging has prompted the claiming and naming of Scottish islands by migrants investing in their western homeland. As people have followed colonization and decolonization which created new waves of reality, trade has been replaced by the trauma of Partition when new borders created fresh displacements of millions of people. The millions did not come to Scotland, but some who found themselves on the 'wrong' side of India's new borders, discovered that they were without a nation overnight, which enforced journeys across the 'black waters' in search of a 'home', which they found in Scotland. The photographs and poems depict the journeys made by itinerant merchants, post-Partition migrants, economic migrants, people moving worlds because of marriage or drawn to Scotland's renowned universities and hospitals.

The sense of uncertainty of the first generation has often been replaced by the confidence of second, third and even fourth generations, educated from the beginning in Scotland and proud to be Scottish. They speak English with Glaswegian or Edinburgh or Fife accents; some speak Gaelic, having appropriated an island culture; they all have the easy agility of jugglers, being naturally bilingual (even trilingual), able to keep their plates spinning in the air. The rhythm of Bhangra, the sparkle of Bollywood, the culinary success of curries, the sophistication of Indian classical music in *ragas* and *talas*, the softness of silks and elegance of eastern fabrics and patterns, have seeped into the Scottish consciousness, bringing a new excitement which is no longer inscrutably Oriental, but has the breath of Indian summers, promising blue skies. The younger generations carry two cultures with them, wearing them like a distinguished paisley pattern, which blends eastern artistry with western expertise. They give their parents a new sense of pride and lend their mothers' once unsure steps, a confident stride. They have owned and applauded their 'broon' inheritance, comfortable in their in-betweenness, as they stride two continents and hold their poise.

And now they have been joined by a fresh group of seekers and surfers, the students and IT personnel who ride a new surging wave of a burgeoning economy and arrive at Scottish Universities and Companies, spill across their market spaces and man supermarket tills and hotel counters at odd hours. This is a generation that will come and go like the ebb and flow of a new tide, forever restless, always ready to leave when new shores open up for their enterprising souls, and at the end of their multiple journeys is the attraction of returning to the land of their ancestors, a modern South Asia that was once the destination of many Scots.

Bashabi Fraser

End Notes

1   Black waters.

2   Prithviraj Chauhan was a king who ruled from the two capitals of Ajmer and Delhi in North India in the 12th century. He is a legendary figure who, it is believed, attended his rival, Raja Jaichand of Kanauj's daughter's (Sanyogita/Sanyukta), swamvara, a ceremony in which the princess chose her husband from amongst the invited guests. Prithviraj was not invited, so he came in disguise. The story goes that he was waiting behind the statue made in his likeness at the gate, which, Sanykta garlanded. He then whisked her away on his horse and married her.

3   A high collared jacket worn by men in South Asia. It is fitted till the waist, widens lower down and comes down to the knees.

4   Chickpea

5   A stringed Indian classical musical instrument.

6   Indian drums

7   A rhythmic cycle, repeated three times.

8   The bells that Indian classical dancers wear on their ankles.

9   A musical composition repeated with variations.

10 A stringed instrument, used as an accompaniment.

11 Ragas form the tonal framework for Indian classical music.

12 Hands used for expressive gestures.

13 Rhythmic cycles.

14 The part of the sari that is thrown over the shoulder.

15 Cumin

16 Meadow

17 Early afternoon prayer on a Friday.

18 A day dedicated to the worship of a particular deity.

19 Ceremonial worship

20 The mountain believed to be the abode of the Hindu pantheon.

21 The Ganges in English.

22 Offering of flowers.

23 Ritual worship performed usually by the priest with earthenware lamps.

24 Journey

25 A small drum.

26 Enrique Miralles was the Spanish architect who led the team who designed the Scottish Parliament.

Some other books published by **LUATH** PRESS

From the Ganga to the Tay: A poetic conversation between the Ganges and the Tay

Bashabi Fraser
ISBN 978-1-906307-95-0 PBK £8.99

The mythical qualities of Indian rivers is profound with daily rituals imprinted in community consciousness. Scotland's rivers were also recognised as the life blood of mother earth, and considered sacred, but cultural evolution seems to have clouded our ancestors' respect for Scotland's most powerful river, the Tay.

KENNY MUNRO

From the Ganga to the Tay is an epic poem in which the Indian River Ganges and the Scottish River Tay, the largest waterways in their countries, relate the historical importance of the ties between India and Scotland. The rivers are potent natural symbols of continuity and peace. With stunning photographs, the conversation between the rivers explores centuries of shared history between Scotland and India as well as each river's personal journey through time.

In the art of Bashabi Fraser the cultures of India and Scotland richly blend, and in this magnificent poem the two living traditions speak to each other through the riverine oracles of the Ganges and the Tay.

RICHARD HOLLOWAY

Tartan and Turban

Bashabi Fraser
ISBN 978-1-842820-44-5 PBK £8.99

Let the powder clouds of Holi – the festival of colour – cover you in purple, pink and green.

Be mesmerised by the proud hooded cobra weaving its charm.

Join a wedding wrapped up in reams of yellow silk and incense and alive with the swish of green kilts and the sound of bagpipes.

Watch the snow melt on the crest of soft dawns and feel the slash of rain against your numb cheek as the wind races across from the North Sea.

Read Bashabi Fraser's poetry and experience a swirl of emotions and images.

A Bengali poet living in Scotland, Bashabi Fraser creatively spans the different worlds she inhabits, celebrating the contrasts of the two countries whilst also finding commonality. Focusing on clear themes and issues – displacement, removal, belonging, identity, war – her poetry is vibrant with feeling and comes alive in an outrageous game of sound patterns.

... mixes up some extraordinarily tasty Indian rhythms with eloquent, Saltire-phile verse.

THE LIST

Tartan & Turban *pulses with youthful vitality that invites readesr to partake of her hospitality, as she mischievously pokes fun at language and the vagaries of her Indo-Scot migrant existence within this well-structured collection. Fraser elegantly dances between the first- and second-generation cultural perspectives, as her enthusiastic writing takes us from West Bengal to London to the Highlands of Scotland.*

SOME MORE POETRY FROM LUATH PRESS

The Luath Kilmarnock Edition: Poems Chiefly in the Scottish Dialect
Robert Burns
ISBN: 978-1-906307-67-7 HBK £15

Merry Muses of Caledonia
Robert Burns
ISBN: 978-1-906307-68-4 HBK £15

Scunnered
Des Dillon
ISBN: 978-1-908373-04-5 PBK £6.99

Dancing with Big Eunice
Alistair Findlay
ISBN: 978-1-906817-28-2 PBK £7.99

The Love Songs of John Knox
Alistair Findlay
ISBN: 978-1-905222-30-8 PBK £7.99

Never Mind the Captions
Alistair Findlay
ISBN: 978-1-906817-89-3 PBK £7.99

Shale Voices
Alistair Findlay
ISBN: 978-1-906307-11-0 PBK £10.99

Kate o Shanter's Tale
Matthew Fitt
ISBN: 978-1-842820-28-5 PBK £6.99

Jane: Poems of a Performance Poet
Anita Govan
ISBN: 978-1-905222-14-8 PBK £6.99

Blind Ossian's Fingal
James Macpherson
ISBN: 978-1-906817-55-8 HBK £15

Love and Revolution
Alastair Mcintosh
ISBN: 978-1-905222-58-2 PBK £8.99

Burning Whins
Liz Niven
ISBN: 978-1-842820-74-2 PBK £8.99

Stravaigin
Liz Niven
ISBN: 978-1-905222-70-4 PBK £7.99

Bad Ass Raindrop
Kokumo Rocks
ISBN: 978-1-842820-18-6 PBK £6.99

Stolen from Africa
Kokumo Rocks
ISBN: 978-1-906307-19-6 PBK £7.99

Bodywork
Dilys Rose
ISBN: 978-1-905222-93-3 PBK £8.99

A Long Stride Shortens the Road
Donald Smith
ISBN: 978-1-842820-73-5 PBK £8.99

Into the Blue Wavelengths
Roderick Watson
ISBN: 978-1-842820-75-9 PBK £8.99

Bunnets 'n' Bowlers
Brian Whittingham
ISBN: 978-1-906307-94-3 PBK £8.99

Drink the Green Fairy
Brian Whittingham
ISBN: 978-1-842820-45-2 PBK £8.99

Accent o the Mind
Rab Wilson
ISBN: 978-1-905222-32-2 PBK £8.99

Life Sentence
Rab Wilson
ISBN: 978-1-906307-89-9 PBK £8.99

A Map for the Blind
Rab Wilson
ISBN: 978-1-906817-82-4 PBK £8.99

The Ruba'iyat of Omar Kayyam in Scots
Rab Wilson
ISBN: 978-1-842820-46-9 PBK £8.99

Details of these and other books published by Luath Press can be found at:
www.luath.co.uk

Luath Press Limited
committed to publishing well written books worth reading

LUATH PRESS takes its name from Robert Burns, whose little collie Luath (*Gael.*, swift or nimble) tripped up Jean Armour at a wedding and gave him the chance to speak to the woman who was to be his wife and the abiding love of his life. Burns called one of 'The Twa Dogs' Luath after Cuchullin's hunting dog in Ossian's *Fingal*. Luath Press was established in 1981 in the heart of Burns country, and is now based a few steps up the road from Burns' first lodgings on Edinburgh's Royal Mile.

Luath offers you distinctive writing with a hint of unexpected pleasures.

Most bookshops in the UK, the US, Canada, Australia, New Zealand and parts of Europe either carry our books in stock or can order them for you. To order direct from us, please send a £sterling cheque, postal order, international money order or your credit card details (number, address of cardholder and expiry date) to us at the address below. Please add post and packing as follows: UK – £1.00 per delivery address; overseas surface mail – £2.50 per delivery address; overseas air-mail – £3.50 for the first book to each delivery address, plus £1.00 for each additional book by airmail to the same address. If your order is a gift, we will happily enclose your card or message at no extra charge.

Luath Press Limited
543/2 Castlehill
The Royal Mile
Edinburgh EH1 2ND
Scotland

Telephone: 0131 225 4326 (24 hours)
Fax: 0131 225 4324
email: sales@luath.co.uk
Website: www.luath.co.uk